Bears, Cannons, Blood and
Why Shakespeare's Theatre was Best

written by Catherine Allison
illustrated by Kathy Baxendale and Nick Schon

Contents

Was Shakespeare's theatre the best?

These are some views people have about the plays of William Shakespeare.

The language is so old-fashioned.

There wasn't any scenery, was there?

The plays are boring!

Why should I want to learn about Shakespeare when he lived hundreds of years ago?

But did you know that if you had gone to the theatre in Shakespeare's day you could have seen:

- 👉 real cannons firing
- 👉 dancing and singing
- 👉 sword fighting
- 👉 fancy costumes
- 👉 great stories
- 👉 heroes, villains and clowns
- 👉 ghosts
- 👉 witches
- 👉 boys dressed as girls pretending to be boys, and
- 👉 statues coming to life?

There were lots of other reasons why it was great fun being part of a theatre audience 500 years ago ...

A great day out

In England in the 1500s, going to the theatre was very popular. Most people couldn't read. There was no television or cinema, so people went to the theatre.

On days when a play was being put on, a flag would fly above the theatre so that people could see it from miles around. In smaller towns, the actors would go through the streets advertising the show.

The Globe Theatre

Just before the play began, a trumpet would sound to tell the audience to hurry to the theatre.

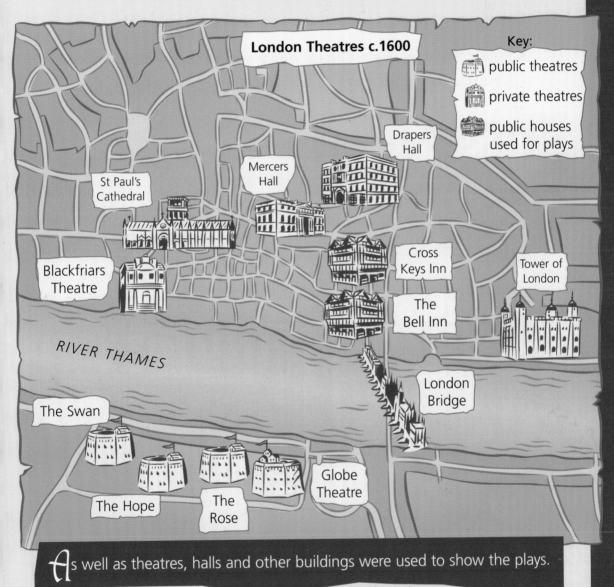

London Theatres c.1600

Key:
- public theatres
- private theatres
- public houses used for plays

Drapers Hall

Mercers Hall

St Paul's Cathedral

Blackfriars Theatre

Cross Keys Inn

The Bell Inn

Tower of London

RIVER THAMES

London Bridge

The Swan

The Hope

The Rose

Globe Theatre

As well as theatres, halls and other buildings were used to show the plays.

There was a **playhouse** of some kind within two miles of every Londoner.

Different types of theatre

There were two types of theatre in Shakespeare's day:

- Public theatres were cheap, noisy and packed with people. The plays were full of action and comedy.

The Globe Theatre was a public theatre.

- Private theatres were smaller. There were fewer people and more comfortable seats.

*B*lackfriars Theatre was a private theatre.

You could go to see plays performed by adult actors. There were also some plays where all the actors were young boys.

Great value for money

In public theatres, you could see a play for less than one penny. The play lasted for two hours or more. Afterwards there was music and dancing.

galleries

groundlings

yard

With a penny ticket you had to stand up in the **yard** in front of the stage. But that was a good place to be because it was very close to the actors. If you stood in the yard you were called a **"groundling"**.

A seat in one of the galleries cost two pence. You could hire a cushion to sit on to make the seat more comfortable.

The richest people paid six pence to sit in a box (called the "lord's room") above the stage.

lord's room

stage

You could be part of the action

In Shakespeare's day, the audience talked all the time! If they enjoyed the acting they clapped and cheered.

If they thought the play was boring, they shouted and threw food at the actors. (Plays were always performed in daylight, so it was easier to hit the actors!)

Exciting stories

Plays in Shakespeare's time had everything that soap operas have today: family arguments and broken friendships, love, jealousy, hatred, violence and mystery.

Hamlet
by W. Shakespeare

Do you believe in ghosts?

... Hamlet, the prince of Denmark, misses his dead father the king and thinks about him all the time. One night, his friends are terrified when they see the ghost of Hamlet's father walking in the castle. It seems that the ghost has a message for his son. At first, Hamlet cannot believe his friends' story, but the following night he decides to see if the ghost will appear and speak to him ...

starring Richard Burbage

Romeo and Juliet
by W. Shakespeare

A pair of star-crossed lovers

Romeo and Juliet are two teenagers in love. Their families hate each other and forbid the lovers to meet. But the lovers will not be kept apart. Juliet's parents try to force her to marry another boy, so she takes a sleeping potion and pretends that she is dead. Romeo finds her asleep and thinks she is really dead. He kills himself. At that very moment, the sleeping potion begins to wear off, and Juliet wakes up ...

starring Edward Alleyn

Lots of different plays

Comedy – A Midsummer Night's Dream

History – Henry V

Some theatres would put on as many as six different plays a week. **Playwrights** could tell which stories were the most popular by counting the number of apple cores thrown at the actors at the end of a show!

The main types of play were:

- Comedies – lighthearted stories with happy endings
- Histories – stories about people from the past, often kings and queens
- Tragedies – stories about powerful people, with sad endings

Quite often, the audience already knew the story of a play when they went to see it.

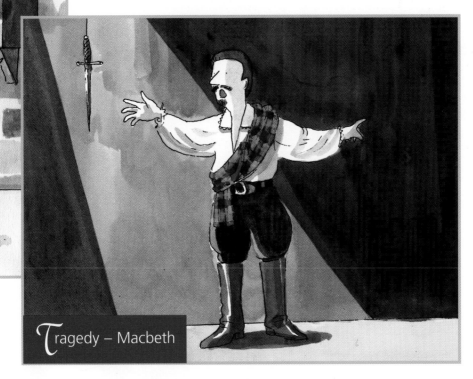

Tragedy – Macbeth

Never a dull moment

Shakespeare wrote comedies, histories and tragedies. He was an actor as well as a playwright, so he knew what audiences liked. He knew they liked stories about wars and battles, mysteries and magic.

The Winter's Tale

The best part was when the statue of Hermione seemed to come to life. It was standing there so still, I never expected anything to happen. Then the statue moved, and beautiful Hermione was alive again. It was magical!

Olivia falls in love with Viola when she is dressed as a boy.

Twelfth Night is my favourite play. Viola dresses as a boy and goes to work for the Duke. He asks her to take messages to Olivia, the woman he loves. Olivia falls in love with Viola, thinking she's a boy. It's very funny because everyone in the audience knows the truth about Viola all the time!

Easy to understand

Plays often started with a **prologue** which told the audience where and when the play was set. When the setting changed, a character spoke to the audience and explained where the scene was taking place. There was no scenery to change, so plays moved fast, from one time to another, or one country to another.

Actors also used **props** to show that the setting had changed. A throne meant the scene was set in a royal palace. A bow and arrows meant hunting in a forest. A painting of the moon meant night time.

Simple clothes meant that the scene had a country setting. Fancy clothes meant the setting was a royal palace or a rich person's home.

This scene from Hamlet takes place in a graveyard. The trapdoor in the stage is used as a grave. Together with the words the actors speak, this is enough to help the audience imagine a real graveyard setting.

Well-designed theatres

Canopy – painted with planets and signs of the zodiac. It had a trapdoor so gods could appear.

Doors – the entrance and exit from the main stage.

Trapdoor – used as a grave, for magical events, or even an entrance to Hell.

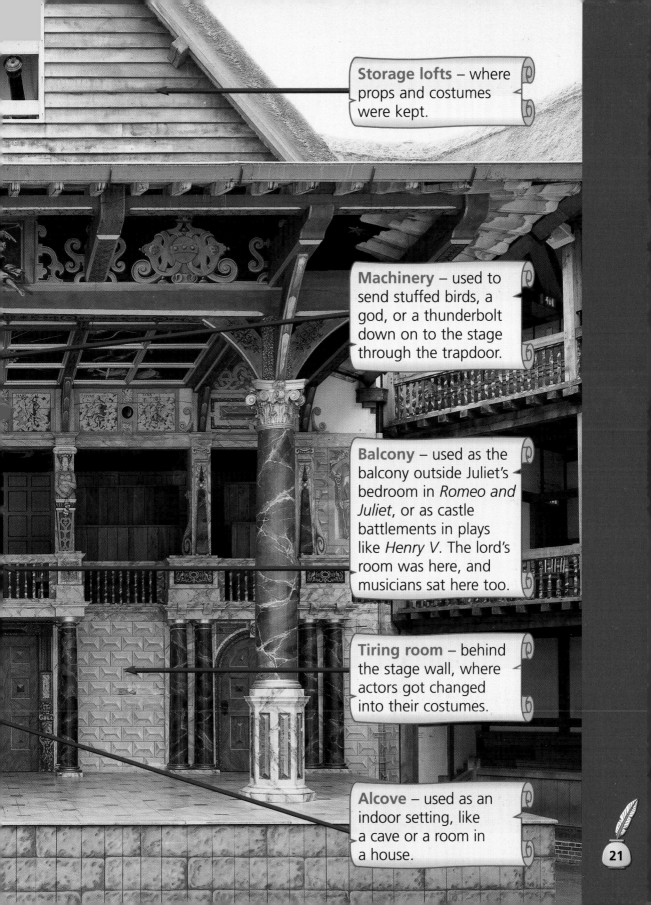

Storage lofts – where props and costumes were kept.

Machinery – used to send stuffed birds, a god, or a thunderbolt down on to the stage through the trapdoor.

Balcony – used as the balcony outside Juliet's bedroom in *Romeo and Juliet*, or as castle battlements in plays like *Henry V*. The lord's room was here, and musicians sat here too.

Tiring room – behind the stage wall, where actors got changed into their costumes.

Alcove – used as an indoor setting, like a cave or a room in a house.

Special effects

Cannons

What could be more exciting in a battle scene than real cannons firing real cannon balls? Cannons were often fired from the roofs of the London theatres during Shakespeare's time. But in 1613, during a performance of the play *Henry VIII*, a cannon was fired and the theatre's thatched roof caught fire. In two hours the whole Globe Theatre had burnt to the ground.

Blood

When an actor was stabbed in a stage fight, he bled real blood! He hid a sponge soaked in animal blood under his shirt. When the sword touched the sponge, the blood came out.

Storms

The theatres used **thundersheets** to make storm noises. Sometimes cannon balls were rolled from side to side to make the right kind of sound.

Bears

There were **bear gardens** in London in Shakespeare's time. Some people think that real brown bears might have been used on the stage. In Shakespeare's play *The Winter's Tale*, one of the stage directions is "Exit pursued by a bear."

Beautiful poetry

Some of the best poetry in English comes from the plays of Shakespeare. He could make you imagine the English countryside.

I know a bank where the wild thyme blows,
Where oxlips and the nodding violet grows,
Quite **over-canopied** with **luscious** woodbine,
With sweet musk-roses, and with eglantine.

A Midsummer Night's Dream

over-canopied overhung
luscious sweet-smelling

He could make you imagine how you would feel before a terrible battle.

> ... when the blast of war blows in our ears,
> Then imitate the action of the tiger;
> Stiffen the **sinews**, summon up the blood,
> Disguise fair nature with **hard-favour'd rage;**
>
> *Henry fifth*

And remember, Shakespeare used the language that people spoke at that time. So the audience would have had no trouble understanding it.

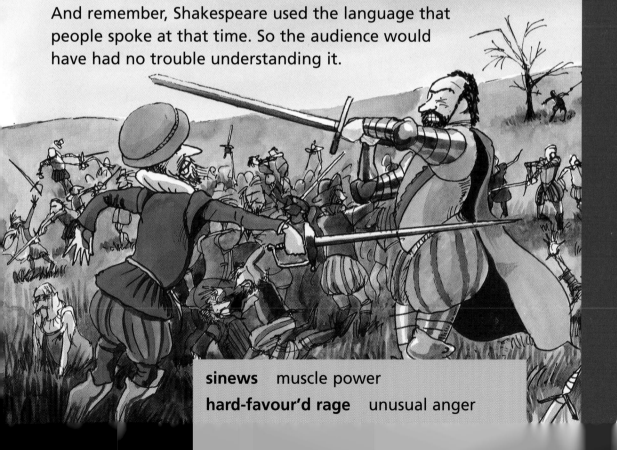

sinews muscle power
hard-favour'd rage unusual anger

Talented actors

At theatres like the Globe, you could see your favourite actors every day of the week. From the 1580s onwards, people went to see star actors, just as people do with films today.

A poster for a modern film version of one of Shakespeare's plays.

Leonardo DiCaprio + Claire Danes

WILLIAM SHAKESPEARE'S
ROMEO + JULIET

Nowadays, people go to the cinema to see famous actors. This poster shows Leonardo di Caprio as Romeo in a modern film adaptation of Romeo and Juliet.

Richard Burbage was a star actor. When he acted the death of Hamlet, the audience and the other actors thought that he was really dying!

Burbage was an actor who also built the Globe Theatre in 1599.

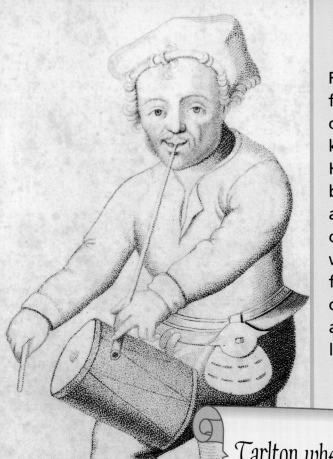

Richard Tarlton was the most famous and popular clown of his time. He was best known for **slapstick** comedy. His jokes were published in a book after he died. He was always introduced by a tune on the pipe and **tabor**. He was so funny that even his face peeping through the curtains could make audiences roar with laughter.

Richard Tarlton.

Tarlton when his head was onely seene,
The **tirehouse** dore and **tapisterie** betweene
Set all the **multitude** in such a laughter,
They could not **hold** for **scarse** an houre after.

tirehouse dressing room
tapisterie curtain
multitude audience
hold stop
scarse nearly

The actors were very good at their jobs. (They had to be, or the audience would throw food at them!)

☞ They had to learn their lines by heart. (Some parts had over 800 lines!)

☞ They had to be able to make their voices heard over the noise from the audience.

☞ They had to be good at fighting on stage. In sword fights, the actors used real swords, so they could not make mistakes.

☞ They had to be able to
sing and, sometimes,
play instruments.

☞ They had to be
able to dance in
different styles.

☞ There were no female
actors on stage until
1660. So young boys
had to be able to act
like girls and women.

Summary

So, do you think you would have enjoyed going to the theatre in Shakespeare's time?

☞ You could have chatted to all your friends, eaten snacks and told the actors what you thought of them.

☞ You could have laughed at the clowns, cried with the victims and hissed at the villains.

☞ You could have seen great special effects.

☞ You could have heard the most beautiful poetry, written by the greatest playwright of all time.

What more could you want for one penny?

Glossary

bear garden   a place where bears were put on show to the public or used for bearbaiting

groundling   one of the audience who stood in the yard

playhouse   a theatre

playwright   someone who writes plays

prologue   an introduction

props   objects used on stage, like cups or swords

tabor   a small drum

thundersheet   a large tin sheet shaken to make storm noise

yard   the area in front of the stage where audience stood

Shakespeare's theatre was the best!

Index

Other titles in the Independent Stage

Geography

Liquid Gold: Water on Tap

Pedal Power: Land's End to John O'Groats in 26 Days

History

Bears, Cannons, Blood and Trumpets: Why Shakespeare's Theatre was Best

Bleak Streets: Victorian London Exposed

Science

Survival Guide

The Story of Scurvy

visit www.literacyland.co.uk
for free activities and fun games

Independent Stage

Bears, Cannons, Blood and Trumpets:

Why Shakespeare's Theatre was Best

Do you think that watching Shakespeare's plays is dull, boring and old fashioned? Then think again! In this book you will learn about the sword fighting, the dancing and the special effects that were part of the performance in Shakespeare's time. Maybe then you will agree that Shakespeare's theatre was the best.

Literacy Land

Info Trail is part of Literacy Land
www.literacyland.co.uk

Pearson Education

ISBN 0-582-77073-4

9 780582 770737